Macaw

E. Melanie Watt

AV2

www.openlightbox.com

1-Year Grades K–5 Subscription
ISBN 978-1-7911-3320-7

Macaw

CONTENTS

Meet the Macaw

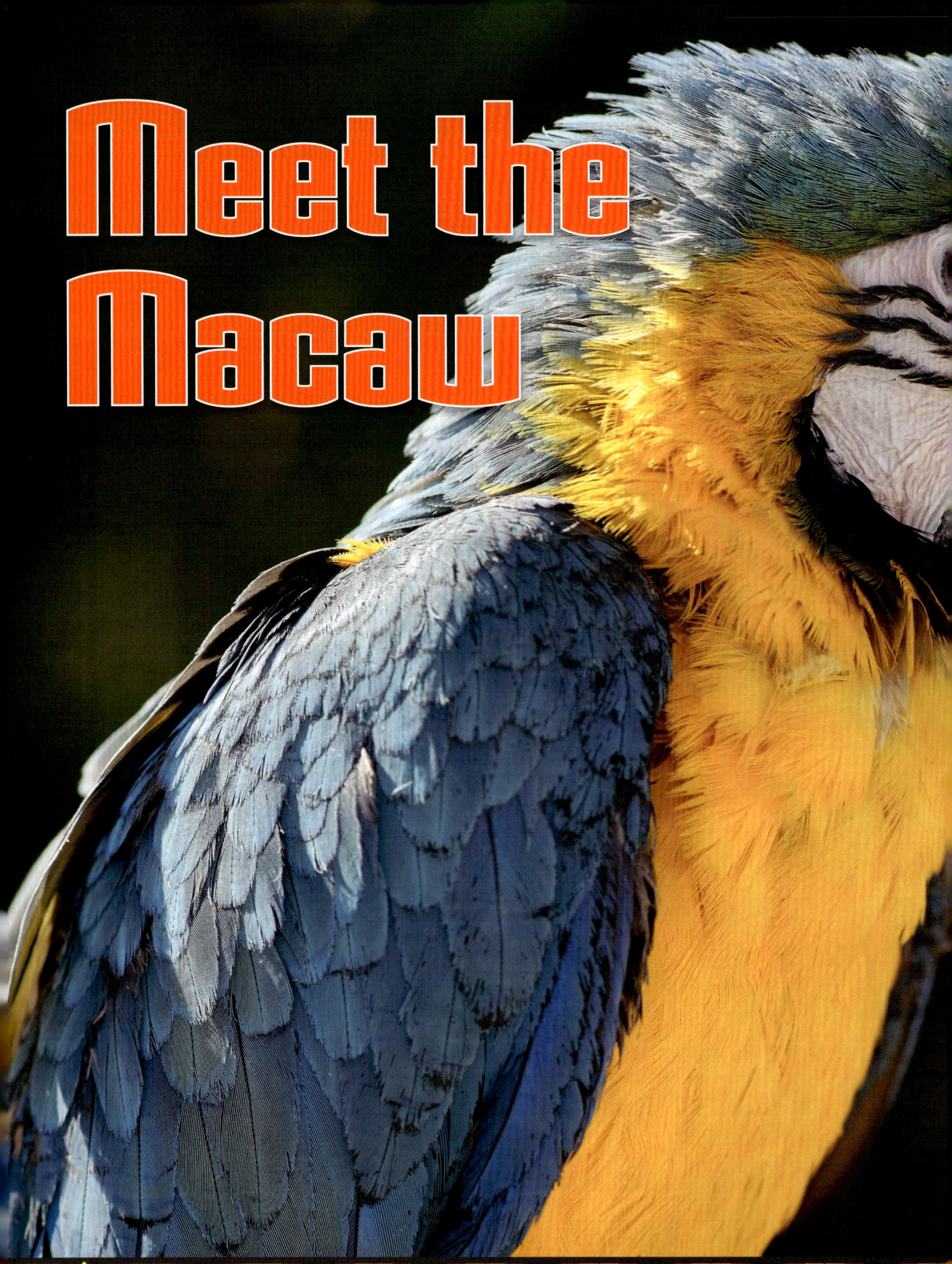

Macaws are large parrots. Many of these birds have brightly colored feathers and patches of bare skin on their faces. Their beaks are strong and curved, and their tails are long and graceful.

Macaws are known for their intelligence as well as their looks. They are noisy and can mimic many sounds. Some even copy human words. This has led to many of these birds being taken and kept as pets.

A Tropical Bird

Macaws live in Mexico, Central America, and South America. Within these areas, they are found in many types of **habitats**, including rainforests. There are at least 17 **species** of macaws. They can be different colors, shapes, and sizes. The largest is the hyacinth macaw. A hyacinth macaw can weigh almost as much as two pineapples.

Social Birds

Depending on the time of year, macaws can live in pairs, family groups, or **flocks** of 10 to 30 birds. Macaws communicate with each other using many different sounds, such as calls, squawks, and screams. A macaw will pair up with one **mate** for life, which can be 60 years or more in nature. The pair share food and groom each other.

Mated macaws will often fly so close together in a flock that their wings almost touch.

Macaw

Growing Up

Macaws make nests in holes in trees or dirt cliffs. Once a macaw mother has laid eggs, she sits on them to keep them warm while the father brings food to the nest. After about 26 days, the young, or chicks, hatch. Their eyes do not open for a few days. They learn to fly when they are about 3 months old, after their feathers grow in.

MACAW FACT

Macaws lay **one to four** eggs at a time.

A Closer Look

Macaws have **adapted** to their habitats. They have unique features that help them survive in their environment.

Tail

A macaw's tail can be as long as its body, or even longer. It helps the bird steer while in flight.

Feet

A macaw has four long toes with sharp claws on each foot. Two toes point forward and two point backward. This arrangement helps macaws hold on to branches and pick up objects.

Ears

A macaw's ears are hidden. The opening hole of each ear is on either side of its head. It is covered with very soft feathers. Macaws use their ears to detect danger and listen for warnings from the flock.

Tongue

A macaw has a dry, somewhat scaly tongue with a bone inside it. The tongue acts as a tool to help the bird reach inside fruit, nuts, and other food.

Beak

Macaws have large, strong, curved beaks. Their beaks help them reach for food and bite through hard fruit and the shells of seeds and nuts.

Blending In

A macaw's feathers come in many shades of green, blue, yellow, red, and other colors. These may help the parrots blend in with tropical forest leaves, brightly colored fruits, and flowers. The colors can also make it difficult for predators to spot one individual bird in a group. Within each species, both male and female macaws are equally colorful.

Male and female macaws look so much alike that people often cannot tell them apart.

Powerful Beaks

Macaw beaks need to be powerful to help the birds bite through the hard shells of their food. The hard covering of their beaks is made from **keratin**. Macaws use their beaks to hold and investigate items. They can also use their beaks to help them climb, treating the beak like an extra foot. Larger macaws tend to have more powerful beaks.

MACAW FACT

Hyacinth macaw beaks can apply more than **300 pounds of pressure per square inch** (2,100 kilopascals). This is enough to break a broom handle in half with one bite.

Macaw

A Wide Diet

Flocks of macaws sleep in trees at night. In the morning, they fly to find food, such as fruit, nuts, seeds, flowers, leaves, insects, and snails. Some foods macaws eat contain toxins that would make other animals sick. To eat these foods, certain macaw species also eat dirt or wet clay, which can remove toxins from their other foods. Another reason macaws may eat clay is because it contains healthy nutrients not found in the rest of their diet.

Hyacinth macaws often eat palm nuts found in cow droppings. They are softer and easier to eat than palm nuts that were not previously eaten by cows.

Macaw Conservation

Several macaw species are **endangered**. Others, such as the Cuban macaw, are **extinct**. A major threat to macaws is when their habitats are destroyed by people. Large numbers of macaws have also been removed from nature by the pet trade and by hunters. Today, many species are protected by law. Spix's macaws have long been **extinct in the wild**. As part of a conservation program, Spix's macaws born in captivity are now being released into their natural habitat.

Eight Spix's macaws were released back into nature on June 11, 2022, in Brazil.

Macaw Conservation Status

EX	EW	CR	EN	VU	NT	LC
Extinct	Extinct in the Wild	Critically Endangered	Endangered	Vulnerable	Near Threatened	Least Concern
Cuban Macaw	Spix's Macaw			Hyacinth Macaw		Northern Red-Shouldered Macaw

Macaw Quiz

1 How many species of macaws are there?

2 What do macaws eat?

3 Which is the world's largest macaw species?

4 Does a macaw have ears?

5 How many eggs do macaws lay at a time?

6 What makes up the hard covering of a macaw's beak?

7 Why might some macaws eat dirt or wet clay?

8 Where do macaws find soft palm nuts?

ANSWERS **1.** At least 17 **2.** Fruit, nuts, seeds, flowers, leaves, insects, and snails **3.** Hyacinth macaw **4.** Yes, ear holes are hidden under soft feathers on each side of its head **5.** One to four **6.** Keratin **7.** To help them digest toxins and to provide healthy nutrients **8.** In cow droppings

Key Words

adapted: changed to suit the environment

endangered: in danger of no longer surviving in the world

extinct: no longer alive anywhere on Earth

extinct in the wild: only living in locations such as zoos

flocks: groups of birds

habitats: places where animals live, grow, and raise their young

keratin: a hard substance that makes up animal body parts including beaks, horns, and claws

mate: a member of a pair of animals that have young

species: a group of related living things that can reproduce

Index

Published by Lightbox Learning Inc.
276 5th Avenue, Suite 704 #917
New York, NY 10001
Website: www.openlightbox.com

Library of Congress Control Number: 2023939839

ISBN 978-1-7911-5698-5 (hardcover)
ISBN 978-1-7911-5697-8 (softcover)
ISBN 978-1-7911-5699-2 (multi-user eBook)

082023
101122

Printed in Guangzhou, China
1 2 3 4 5 6 7 8 9 0 27 26 25 24 23

Project Coordinator: Priyanka Das
Art Director: Terry Paulhus

Every reasonable effort has been made to trace ownership and to obtain permission to reprint copyright material. The publisher would be pleased to have any errors or omissions brought to its attention so that they may be corrected in subsequent printings.

The publisher acknowledges Alamy, Bridgeman Images, Dreamstime, Minden Pictures, and Shutterstock as its primary image suppliers for this title.